Versions and Verses.

BY

CHARLES DEXTER.

CAMBRIDGE:
SEVER AND FRANCIS.
1865.

UNIVERSITY PRESS:
WELCH, BIGELOW, AND COMPANY,
CAMBRIDGE.

TO ONE GONE.

CONTENTS.

VERSIONS.

VERSES.

VERSIONS.

NOAH'S ARK.

W. MÜLLER.

THAT Adam ate, not that he drank,
Was he from Eden's garden driven;
And what he lost by eating then
To us anew by wine is given;
Yes! wine restores those Eden days,
So here 's to wine and jolly lays!

And when once more throughout the world,
By baser appetite betrayed,
Man only thought what he would eat,
And gluttony alone prevailed,
The Deluge came, to cure the ill,
But Noah spared, the vine to till.

Aboard a mighty cask he went,
It bore him high above the tide ;
And many jolly days and nights
He rolled across the waters wide ;
What kept old Noah safe and sound ?
Why wine, not water, I 'll be bound !

Subsided now the angry flood,
The gallant house, so round and tight,
Stuck fast upon a mountain-top :
I' faith, it was a goodly sight !
And Noah went, with heart elate,
The hill to plant with luscious grape.

And there upon the mountain-top
To-day that very ark is seen,
In Heidelberg, on the Neckar,
The giant tun of tuns, I ween :
So now we know who gave the vine
To those who dwell along the Rhine.

If any mortal rash should dare
To cast a slur on wine divine,
Toss him in the depths of ocean,
And let him pickle in the brine!
While we enjoy our Eden-days,
And drink, — and sing our jolly lays!

DEAD HOPES.

W. MÜLLER.

HERE and there upon the tree
A leaf may yet be seen,
And oft and oft beneath the tree,
In deep and pleasant reverie,
I stand, lost in a dream.

Long I gaze upon the leaf,
There hang my hopes so high ;
And when the wind plays with my leaf,
In fear I tremble, — and the leaf
Scarce trembles more than I.

Ah! should fall the leaf to earth,
Then fall my hopes so high!
I bow my stricken head to earth,
And weep o'er hopes dead in the birth,
That seemed too fair to die!

WANDERING.

W. MÜLLER.

TO wander is the miller's joy,
To wander!
He must a wretched miller be
Who never longed to wander free,
To wander!

From water we 've the lesson learnt,
From water!
It resteth not by day or night,
To wander ever thinketh right,
Doth water!

And so the wheels go round and round,
The water-wheels!
They love not ever still to be,
Revolving fast, revolving free,
The water-wheels!

The pebbles e'en tho' hard they seem,
The pebbles !
They gayly spin in circlets round,
And long to go with quicker bound,
The pebbles !

To wander ! wander ! is my joy,
To wander !
Good master and good mistress true,
Let me depart in peace from you,
To wander !

THE MILLER'S SONG.

W. MÜLLER.

WHERE'ER a heart, o'ercome by love
Neglected, dies,
The lilies mourn with drooping head,
And downcast eyes.

The sorrowing moon will shine no more
With silver light,
But veils her weeping face in clouds
From human sight.

In Heaven all the angel host,
With brimming eyes,
Sob and sing the soul to its rest
In Paradise.

In yon bright dome another star
Sheds its mild light,
There, disenthralled, the spirit reigns
A gem of night.

. . . . .

A SWEETHEART EVERYWHERE.

W. MÜLLER.

I 'VE a sweetheart by the Rhine,
Another by the Spree,
A third away in Switzerland,
A fourth upon the sea.

Where'er I go, where'er I stay,
In castle, town, or hall,
I find a sweetheart ever there,
The loveliest of all.

Wouldst comprehend my cunning art,
Ye wandering friends of mine?
Come, gather round, and listen all,
I 'll tell it in a line.

I carry ever in my breast
  My sweetheart loved of all;
And so forever she goes too
  To castle, town, or hall.

Welcome! darling by the Rhine!
  How far is 't to the sea?
Farewell! sweetheart in Switzerland!
  Parting 's nothing to me!

THE INQUIRER.

W. MÜLLER.

NOT of the bright, gay-tinted flowers,
Nor stars that twinkle so,
Have I the question ever asked
That I would gladly know.

I know not what the flowers say;
Too high the starry throng;
I 'll ask the little rivulet
If my heart tells me wrong.

Ah! murm'ring, shining rivulet,
Why art thou now so dumb?
O prithee speak, and answer me,
One little word, — but one.

Is 't Yes or No? how small the word
  That I would beg from thee!
Yet Yes or No indeed is more
  Than all the world to me!

Sweet murm'ring, glancing rivulet,
  Thy talk is mystery:
I pray thee stop, O stop, and say,
  Has she no love for me?

IF THE LITTLE FLOWERS KNEW.

HEINE.

KNEW the tender little flowers
Of the wound deep in my heart,
They would weep within their bowers,
And a comfort would impart.

Could the nightingales imagine
Half my sorrow, grief, and wrong,
They would softly, sweetly warble
In a more melodious song.

Knew the meek-eyed stars in Heaven
Of my bitterness and woe,
They would stoop to whisper gently
Consolation here below.

Ah! but these — they cannot know it!
  There 's but one who knows my pain; —
She indeed — the cruel maiden —
  She has rent my heart in twain!

THE OLD STORY.

HEINE.

ONCE was an aged king;
His heart was stern, his hair was gray;
And took this aged king
A fair young wife, one day.

Once was a handsome page;
Gold were his locks, lightsome his air;
Bore he the silken train
Of one as frail as fair.

Dost know the oft-told tale?
It sounds so sweet, it sounds so fell,
Must die both queen and page:
Alas! they loved too well!

2

LOVE'S TEARS.

HEINE.

I WEPT, dreaming
  That thou wert dead!
I woke, weeping, —
  And still tears shed.

I wept, dreaming
  That thou hadst gone!
I woke, weeping, —
  And still wept on.

I wept, dreaming
  Thou wert true to me!
I woke, weeping, —
  Tears constantly!

LOVE'S ANXIETY.

HEINE.

AS a beautiful flower,
Pure, lovely, thou art;
I gaze on thee, — sorrow
Steals over my heart.

I long, why I know not,
Our Saviour to pray
To keep thee as lovely,
As stainless alway.

THE ERRAND.

HEINE.

UP, laggard! arise, and saddle in haste
The fleetest steed in the stall,
And ride for dear life over forest and field,
To King Duncan's lordly Hall!

Await at the gate till there comes to thee
Some one of his serving train,
Then ask him at once, "Quick! tell me which weds,
Which one of the daughters twain?"

And if he replies, "'T is the dark-eyed one,"
Then haste with all speed to me;
But if he replies, "'T is the fair-eyed maid,"
Ride back to me leisurely.

Stop as thou comest so leisurely back,
  And buy me a rope right stout,
And slowly ride home, but say not a word
  Of what thou hast been about!

THE VOICE OF THE MOUNTAIN.

HEINE.

A RIDER goes through the silent vale,
He is sad, and his pace is slow:
"Alas! am I going to my loved one,
Or down to the grave so low?"
The voice of the mountain echo
Said, "Down to the grave so low!"

And farther the horseman sad rode on,
And he sighed from a heart of woe,
"If down to the grave I must wend my way,
O there, there is peace, I know!"
The voice of the mountain echo
Said, "There, there is peace, I know!"

Adown the face of the rider fell
  A tear from the fount of his woe:
"If but in the grave the weary may rest,
  'T is best to the grave to go!"
  The voice of the mountain echo
  Said, "Best to the grave to go!"

A VENETIAN TRIAD.

A. GRÜN.

I 'D wish, if wishing aught availed,
Three things were mine :
A maiden fair, a priest of Rome,
A gondel fine.

" Say, wherefore now the maiden fair ? "
" Then we were two :
Alone to sigh, alone to pray,
This one can do ! "

" Say, wherefore now the priest of Rome ? "
" Lest sin ensue :
No one can say what might befall,
Where there are two ! "

"Say, wherefore now the gondel fine?"
  "That I might glide
From maiden quick to priest, and back
  To her dear side."

THE BUD IN THE BOOK.

A. GRÜN.

AN old and palsied aunt have I,
 A little book has she :
Within the book, the leaves atween,
 A withered bud I see.

And withered too indeed the hands
 That plucked it years long past :
What grief disturbs that aged one ?
 She sees it, — tears fall fast !

THE LAST POET.

A. GRÜN.

"WHEN, O ye Poets, will ye
  Cease singing on and on?
When will at last be ended
  The old, eternal song?

"Have ye not long since sounded
  The last melodious strain?
Still find ye flowers to gather,
  And fountains still to drain?"

"Long as the Sun, the day-god,
  Through heaven drives his car;
And but one human visage
  May watch him from afar.

"Long as the storm-king rages
  Along the lightning's path ;
And one faint heart, in terror,
  Bows down before his wrath.

"Long as the archéd rainbow
  Springs when the torrents cease ;
And fills one mortal bosom
  With hope and blesséd peace.

"Long as the night the ether
  Sows with her starry seed ;
And yet, on earth, one being
  The golden writ may read.

"Long as the moon may shine on
  One full and longing breast ;
Long as the forest offers
  The weary traveller rest.

"Long as the spring may blossom
  With gayest garden hues;
Long as cheeks may bloom, and eyes
  The light of joy diffuse.

"Long as the gloomy cypress
  Its moan by graves may make;
Long as eye hath power to weep,
  And heart hath cause to break.

"So long on earth there wanders
  The goddess Poesie!
And with her one, rejoicing
  Her chosen priest to be.

"And singing, and rejoicing
  Through all this mortal sphere,
When dies the last of poets,
  Then dies the last man here!

"God holds this fair creation,
  A flower in His hand,
Fresh, pure, and brightly blooming,
  And smiles upon the land.

"When withered is the flower,
  And crushed and dead it lies,
And earth, and sun, and heaven
  Are blotted from our eyes,

"Then ask, if yet desirous
  The truth to know, how long
Before at last 't is ended,
  The old, eternal song!"

MAN'S TEARS.

A. GRÜN.

MAIDEN! thou hast seen me weeping!
Ah! the tears of woman flow
Like the gentle dews from heaven,
Bidding flowers fairer glow!

Whether night has sadly wept them,
Or with smiling morn they fall,
Yet the dews the flowers freshen
Into bloom and beauty all.

But the tears of man resemble
Precious sap of Eastern tree:
Deep within the bark enhidden,
Flowing secretly, yet free.

Far beneath the rough rind cutting
  To the inmost heart anear,
So the noble sap, outpouring,
  Flows then golden, pure, and clear.

Soon indeed the fount may dry up,
  And the tree wax strong and green,
Many another springtide greeting ;
  Yet the cut, the wound is seen.

Maiden ! of the tree bethink thee,
  On the top of Eastern steep !
Maiden ! of the man bethink thee,
  Whom thou saw'st once to weep !

THE SOURCE OF SONG.

A. GRÜN.

WHY is 't that with the arrow in the heart
The rankling soul breaks into song?
Why is 't that from a breast nigh torn apart
Wakes music that has slumbered long?

The snow-white plumaged swan majestic floats
Upon the bosom of the tides,
Through all his sunny summer life, no notes
Of song, as mute he onward glides.

At early blush of morn, at moonlight pale,
Voiceless he sailed, and never sang:
Where Spring with varied flowers strewed the vale,
He floated by, but never sang.

But now that thou an arrow in his breast
　　Hast drove, and Death is creeping on,
All that could find no voice at Joy's behest
　　Bursts forth in sorrow and in song.

WREATHS.

A. GRÜN.

OFT the bridal wreath has blossomed
  In the church-yard's fertile earth :
Round the head of bride still whispering
  Of the grave that gave it birth.

Oft the funeral wreath hath blossomed
  In the garden's fairy ring :
Round the head of corpse still whispering
  Of its tender nurse, the Spring.

CONTRADICTION.

A. GRÜN.

WHEN on thy cherry lips I hung,
And drank the perfume of thy breath,
I dreamt of parting, and of woe,
And dreamt of thee, as cold in death.

And now, as by thy grave I stand,
I dream but of Love's time of bliss,
Of cheeks that rivalled e'en the rose,
And of thy long, impassioned kiss.

DISSIMILAR SORROW.

A. GRÜN.

BESIDE a grave, on bended knee,
A maiden plants a poplar-tree :
" O Poplar ! grow towards the sky ;
Released, his spirit soared on high ;
To Heaven every twig incline,
As prayer points these hands of mine :
Towards the stars each leaf arise,
As thither turn my longing eyes :
To him ! to him ! above ! above !
May'st grow a monument of love ;
So planted on his grave, O tree,
The image of my sorrow be ! "

Beside a grave, on bended knee,
A sad youth plants a willow-tree :

"O willow! grow towards the ground,
She lies beneath this grassy mound:
  Drip gentle dews upon her head,
As on her grave my tears are shed:
  And in thy leafy arms enfold
The form that Death snatched from my hold:
  To her! to her! below! below!
A monument of love may'st grow;
  So planted on her grave, O tree,
  The image of my sorrow be!"

LENORE.

BÜRGER.

AT dawn Lenore rose from bed,
From horrid dream awakened, —
"Art faithless, Wilhelm, or art dead,
Thus long am I forsakened?"
With royal Fred'rick's armèd train,
He went upon the Prague campaign,
And never had he sent her
A token, word, or letter.

The Monarch and the Empress both,
Aweary of the struggle,
Had made a peace, and ta'en an oath
To end the war and trouble:

And troops, with cheers that ring and rang,
With trumpet blasts that cling and clang,
  Begirt with laurel chaplet,
  Return to town and hamlet.

And everywhere, O, everywhere,
  By every path outpouring,
Went old and young, rejoicing there
  To hail the troops returning;
"Thank God!" each child and mother cried,
"O welcome!" sobbed each happy bride.
  For poor Lenore tearful,
  No kiss, or greeting cheerful.

She questioned every one she met,
  A thousand times she named him,
No word of Wilhelm did she get,
  Not one she found who knew him:
And when the troops had all marched past,
  Her raven hair she tore at last,

And on the ground prostrated,
She raved and imprecated.

Her mother hurried to her side,
"O God! have pity on her!
Child of my heart! what is 't?" she cried,
And threw her arms about her.
"O mother! mother! all is lost!
To me the world and all is lost!
God looks in scorn upon me!
God has no pity for me!"

"O help us now! Good Lord! be kind!
Child! say a pater-noster:
God tempers to the lamb the wind,
And us his care will foster."
"O mother! mother! God 's unkind!
He tempers not to me the wind;
Of what avail is prayer?
When did it help the sayer?"

"God help us now! who knows the Lord
  Knows he is good in sorrow:
The sacrament will sure afford
  A comfort you may borrow."
"O mother! mother! my tormènt
Will ease no blessèd sacrament,
  No sacrament can ever
  Restore the dead forever!"

"O listen, child! what if your dear,
  In Hungary delaying,
Forgets the troth he plighted here,
  With some new love remaining?
Bewail him then no more, my child,
Forget him, and be reconciled;
  Whoso his oath has broken,
  The Devil hath bespoken."

"O mother! mother! lost is all!
  Lost, lost, all is forever!

Death, Death, on thee I fain would call :
  Would I had been born never!
O hateful life, quench quick thy light
In all the horror of Death's night.
  God looks in scorn upon me!
  God has no pity for me!"

"God help us now! O, judge her not,
  Thy poor, poor, sinful creature!
All she has said, she has forgot,
  Thy piety, O, teach her!
O child! cease from thy sinfulness,
And turn to God and blissfulness,
  And he will fail you never,
  His love endures forever!"

"O mother! what is blissfulness?
  And, mother! what is Hell?
With him, with him, is blissfulness!
  Without him, that is Hell!

O hateful life, quench quick thy light
In all the horror of Death's night;
  For me all bliss soever
  Is gone on Earth forever!"

So raved she there, in wild despair,
  Her reason all dethronèd:
Presuming 'gainst God's will to dare,
  The while her loss she moanèd:
She wrung her hands, her bosom beat,
Till purple day fell fast asleep,
  And night the ether sprinkled
  With starry gems that twinkled.

When, hark! without comes trap, trap, trap,
  Like hoof of steed resounding,
And down a rider leapt to rap,
  Upon the knocker pounding:
And list, and list, the hammer-tap
Goes up and down, rap-rap, rap-rap,

And ere the door they open,
These words distinct are spoken :

" Hollo ! Hollo ! come ope to me !
Dost wake or sleep, my darling ?
Dost dream and wonder where I be,
Dost laugh or weep, my darling ? "
" Ah Wilhelm, thou ! so late at night,
I 've wept and watched till wearied quite,
With sorrow agitated :
Whence com'st thou so belated ? "

" We saddled not till dead of night,
From far Bohemia starting ;
'T is late : but I must fain alight,
To take with me my darling."
" Come in, Wilhelm, 't is bitter cold,
The wind is whistling down the wold,
Come in, and let me fold you,
O best beloved, and warm you ! "

" O let the wind sweep down the wold,
  What though it rage, arousèd !
My steed is restive, uncontrolled,
  Not here can I be housèd !
Come, rise, and up behind me spring,
Upon the steed I 've here waiting ;
  Far must we ride, my darling,
  To bridal bed, ere morning ! "

" So many miles, alas ! ere thou
  Canst bring me to the bride bed ?
Hark to the chimes that echo now,
  'T is eleven has just soundèd."
" See here! see there! the moon shines bright,
We and the dead ride fast to-night !
  A wager I will lead thee
  Where bridal bed awaits thee."

" Now, Wilhelm, where 's thy dwelling, say,
  And what the bridal bed is ? "

" Still, cool, and small, but far away,
  Of eight smooth boards it made is."
" And room for me ? " " For thee and me !
Spring up behind, and thou shalt see :
  The guests have been bespoken,
  The chamber door is open."

Lenore rose, sprang up in haste
  To seat secure behind him :
The rider held, in tight embrace,
  Her arms thrown round about him ;
And hurry, hurry, hop, hop, hop,
Away they sped, in wild gallòp ;
  More fleet than storm they travel,
  'Mid cloud of sparks and gravel.

And right and left, on either hand,
  Before her vision dazzled,
How flew the hedges and the land,
  And how the bridges rattled !

"Art frightened, dear? the moon shines bright;
Hurrah! the dead ride fast to-night!
Does my darling fear the dead?"
"No! O, speak not of the dead!"

What bell, what strain in air does pant,
What flapping wing of raven!
Hark! tolling bell! hark! burial chant!
A soul has found its haven:
And nearer drew a funeral train,
The hearse and body nearer came,
And a priest who walked ahead
Said the service for the Dead.

"At midnight's close, that body hide,
With wail and chant sepulchral;
Home now I take my tender bride;
Come to the bridal festal!
Come, sexton, here, and your choir bring,
Bid them their best bride-choral sing,

And thou, O Priest, come bless us,
Ere in our bed we lay us!"

The chant is hushed; the mourners past,
Obedient to his bidding,
Turn face about, and follow fast
Behind the rider grinning:
And further, further, hop, hop, hop,
Along they flew in wild gallòp,
More fleet than storm they travel,
'Mid cloud of sparks and gravel.

How flew to right, how flew to left,
Huts, towns, and habitations:
How flew to left, and right, and left,
Woods, mountains, and plantations!
"Art frightened, dear? the moon shines bright;
Hurrah! the dead ride fast to-night!
Does my darling fear the dead?"
"O, disturb them not, the dead!"

Look here! look there! a gallows round
  In maddened circle whirling,
There danced a roaring mob around
  About a victim twirling:
"Ho! mob! ho! with shout and laughter,
Join the crowd that follows after,
  A wedding dance shalt dance us,
  Ere in our bed we lay us!"

And headlong rushed the mob along
  Behind him, howling, groaning;
As when the blustering winds blow long,
  Amid the dead leaves moaning:
And further, further, hop, hop, hop,
Ahead they sped in wild gallòp;
  More fleet than storm they travel,
  'Mid cloud of sparks and gravel.

And round and round the full moon spun,
  Afar in space behind them;

The sky, with swinging star-lamps hung,
Sped far away behind them :
"Art frightened, dear? the moon shines bright;
Hurrah! the dead ride fast to-night!
Does my darling fear the dead?"
"Yes! O let them rest, the dead."

"Steed! steed! did not the cock crow there?
Wellnigh the sands are drained :
Steed! steed! I snuff the morning air,
Steed! be no more detained!
Complete! complete is our journèy, —
And there the bridal bed I see;
The dead! how fast they travel,
Here is at last our hostel!"

Towards the iron barrèd grate
They rushed with speed of lightning;
The double doors swung open straight,
No need of their alighting :

At touch, bolt, bar, shot back with jar,
A graveyard stretched before them far,
  And in the moon's cold glimmer
  The headstones seemed to shiver.

Ha! look! a single instant, and,
  O horror! what a wonder!
The breastplates parted band by band,
  Like rotten wood asunder!
Where was a head, a skull behold,
The flesh and hair all turned to mould:
  There ghastly grinned anext her,
  With scythe and glass, the spectre!

The snorting steed leapt high in air,
  There fell a shower of fire:
He disappears amid the glare, —
  The flames alike expire:
A fearful howl comes down the sky,
The dead arise where'er they lie,

Lenore's soul a-quaver,
'Twixt life and death doth waver!

When, in the moonbeam's spectral ray,
A troop of horrid spectre
Begin to dance, and, howling, say
These words, when they come next her:
"*Be patient, though the heart do break:*
What God wills, suffer for His sake;
Now thy body's knell we toll,
God have mercy on thy soul!"

BEAUTIFUL SUE.

BÜRGER.

LONG time I knew the lovely Sue,
  How beautiful was she !
Her modesty and virtues too
  I could not fail to see.
I came and went, and went and came,
  Like tide, in ebb and flow,
With pleasure always when I came,
  Nor sorrowing to go.

And after-while it came to pass
  A change stole over me,
It gave me pain to go, alas !
  And joy with her to be.
She grew the darling of my life,
  My thought by day, by night,

With her my being all was rife,
  My pole-star, beaming bright.

And then I grew dull, dumb, and shy!
  One filled my soul, 't was she!
No bloom or beauty caught my eye,
  She only bloomed for me!
Nor sun, nor moon, nor star gave light,
  While she resplendent shone:
Whene'er she passed before my sight,
  She dazzled me, I own.

And finally it came to pass
  That all was changed again,
Not less my darling was the lass,
  As beauteous did remain:
I came and went, and went and came,
  Like tide, in ebb and flow,
With pleasure always when I came,
  Nor sorrowing to go.

Ye Sages, thought to be aware
  Of all below, above,
When, how, and where do two hearts pair,
  What is this bond of Love?
Ye learned Sages, answer, pray,
  Explain, I beg of ye,
When, how, and where Love makes his way,
  And why this happened me?

I've thought it o'er by day, by night,
  And night and day again,
To solve the riddle if I might,
  But I have thought in vain:
For Love is like the wind at sea,
  You feel its breath, I know,
But can you tell whence comes it free,
  Or whither it will blow?

WINTER-SONG.

BÜRGER.

DECEMBER'S cold and cruel hand
  Has stript the poplar-tree :
In all the bare and shrivelled land,
  No jocund May I see :
And flow'rets red, and white, and blue,
'Neath snow and ice are lost to view.

But, flow'rets dear, expect not me
  To make a dirge my song :
For true to me yon maid I see,
  Whose beauty is lifelong !
More white her skin, more blue her eye,
More red her lip, than ye, or sky !

Wherefore bewail the dove in vale,
  Or Philomel in grove,
If Molly's song do never fail
  Of music that I love?
Her breath, as sweet as breath of Spring,
Has fragrance more than flowers bring!

Whene'er her purple lip I touch,
  A moment 's gone, of bliss!
No berry, cherry, has so much
  Of nectar as her kiss!
O May! why need I long for thee,
With Spring and Molly both by me!

THE SERENADE.

UHLAND.

"WHAT heard I while dreaming,
What wakens me sleeping,
Such music divine?
Look forth, O, I pray thee!
Look forth, and O tell me
Whence 't is, mother mine!"

"I see and I hear naught,
Sleep on then and dream not,
My poor stricken one!
No serenade near thee,
No one but me with thee,
And the night nearly done!"

"Not of earth — not of earth,
But of heavenly birth,
  This music divine!
They call me! they call me, —
The angels do call me, —
  Good night! mother mine!"

PROMISE OF SPRING.

UHLAND.

ALL day, all night, the linden bloom
Breathes tenderly a sweet perfume
Through shady dell, o'er mellow plain ;
O fragrance fair!
O luscious air!
Then, my poor heart, come, rest from care!
Past grief and pain,
O, smile again!

The earth shall fairer grow each day,
How fair, what word will fitly say?
For everywhere a bloom shall reign :

Each spot, yet bare,
Shall beauty wear;
Then, my poor heart, O rest from care!
Past grief and pain,
O, smile again!

THORILDE'S SONG.

UHLAND.

ALONE sat by the sea-shore green,
  With rod and line, a maid;
But though she sat there long, I ween,
  No fish her pains repaid.

A ring from off her hand she took,
  A ring with jewels fine;
Baiting therewith her slender hook,
  Again she cast her line.

When lo! there rose from out the sea
  A hand as iv'ry fair,
And on the hand shone brilliantly
  The ring with jewels rare.

And then there rose from out the sea
  A knight so young, so fair,
In golden armor clad, shone he
  Full in the sun-light there.

Shudd'ring, the maiden shrieked with fear:
  "No, noble knight! O, no!
Restore my golden ring so dear,
  With thee I would not go!"

"Maiden! they catch no fishes here
  With costly jewels rare!
Mine forever the ring so dear,
  And mine art thou fore'er!"

THE LANDLADY'S DAUGHTER.

UHLAND.

THREE travellers journeyed over the Rhine,
And all three stopped at an inn to dine.

"Good Landlady, have you wine and beer,
And why is thy daughter fair not here?"

"Right cool is my wine, my beer is sweet;
But my daughter fair sleeps Death's last sleep."

Now into the room they softly tread,
There lies the poor maiden, cold and dead.

The first, the veil from her face he took,
And gazed on the maid with mournful look.

"Alas! if thou couldst but living be,
From this day forward I'd love but thee!"

The second, he did the veil replace,
And tearfully turned aside his face.

"Alas that thou art on Death's cold bier,
For I have loved thee many a year!"

The third, he removed once more the veil,
And kissed the dead maiden's lips so pale.

"I have loved thee e'er, — still love but thee, —
I'll love thee now, till Eternity!"

THE NUN.

UHLAND.

IN the quiet cloister gardens,
'Neath the sad moon's pallid rays,
Walks a weary maiden, weeping
O'er the love of other days.

" Well for me that my dear lover
On the earth no more I see,
Wasting with a love denied :
Now an angel, he may love me,
I may be his angel-bride!"

Weary as she comes a-weeping
To the holy Virgin's shrine,
Radiant in the moonbeams bright

Stands the mother meek, benign,
Pointing up to realms of light.

At her feet, the maiden sinking,
Finds a comfort in her breast,
Gently breathes her life away;
The broken heart, fore'er at rest,
Rejoices in eternal day!

LOVE IS DUMB.

GEIBEL.

DOST ask me, darling of my soul,
  Why dumb this tongue of mine?
It is because love thronèd sits, —
  All queenly sits,
  In my heart's shrine.

When fiercely mount the flames the sky,
  Nor brook a human will,
They flap their fiery wings on high, —
  So wild and high,
  And yet so still.

Nor ever speaks the rose a word,
  When ope its eyes to light,

But glows, and breathes a sweet perfume, —
  A sweet perfume,
  O'er beauteous night.

So 't is indeed with my fond love,
  Since one bent over me;
It glows, and blooms deep in my heart, —
  Deep in my heart,
  All silently!

HOW STRANGE THE HEART!

GEIBEL.

I often despair of the human heart,
  So strange its power,
That sorrow and joy alike are forgot,
  In one passing hour!

No matter how fond the heart, and how true,
  That woes chastise:
Again the bird sings, the sun shines anew,
  And afar woe flies!

No matter how bright the joy, and how deep:
  Let one cloud arise,
Forgotten at once all memories sweet
  Of our Paradise!

When I consider, I scarcely can say
  Which startles me more, —
That Joy, so swift winged, flies quickly away,
  Or grief 's so soon o'er!

THE BRIDE'S SAIL.

EICHENDORFF.

FROM yonder castle by the sea,
  That breasts the waves below,
Float strains of festive melody;
  And, under lights aglow,
There gayly moves a wedding throng
The measures of the dance among.

But at an archèd window there,
  (He would not join the rout,)
The bridegroom gazed across the wave,
  And watched the stars come out:
The Ocean's spell fell o'er his soul,
The while he eyed its restless roll.

And tenderly the fearless knight
Addressed his beauteous bride:
"Soft breathes the music o'er the night;
In storms alone 's my pride!
And when the winds blow furious, mad,
And Ocean rages, — then I 'm glad!

"I cannot idly loiter here
The level sands about:
This wall of rock, that rises drear,
Fills with despair and doubt;
And yonder stars are telling me
Of distant lands, O fair to see!

"Canst thou have faith, and wilt thou dare,
Like Argonaut of yore,
The glorious waves will kindly bear
Thee to a wondrous shore:
I must contend with wave and wind,
Ere I the home I long for find!

"And there are wings for earnest souls
In yon sails flitting by;
And hear you how old Ocean trolls
His song of melody?
O let such be thy wedding song!
Wilt come, wilt come with me along?

"If thou dost really love me so,
Say yes, nor hesitate;
From castle, garden, you must go,
Leave parents desolate:
Upon the sea, with me alone,
Then art thou, only then, my own!"

He gazed upon her trustful face,
With all love's blessèd glow;
She sank, o'erwhelmed, in his embrace,
And, tearful, murmured low:
"To thee I did my fate confide,
My life, when I became thy bride!"

With joy he bore her down the hill,
  To the boat upon the shore:
The wedding guests expect them still, —
  Vain to await them more.
Faint dies the music on the breeze,
Around them rise and fall the seas.

When dimly in the blushing brine
  The stars faint mirrored are,
And high the sun begins to climb,
  The shore they left is far;
The drunken waves, in riotous play,
The bark drive swiftly on its way.

Moon after moon the bark sped swift,
  Strange winds their faces kissed;
They saw an island vision drift,
  A cloud with purple mist;
And, tinged with every rainbow hue,
Strange birds athwart their pathway flew.

A joyful shiver coursed their veins,
  But ruthless swept the sea!
The wind's breath, like a hurricane's,
  Blew up and down the sea!
While, 'mid the storm, the knight steadfast
The rudder held, with fearless grasp.

Wild lightnings flashed from out the sky;
  The sea boiled o'er the rocks;
When, borne upon a wave-crest high,
  The boat split on the rocks;
And stagg'ring from the splintered mast,
The loving knight his bride held fast!

His frighted burden close embraced,
  He leaped into the sea;
Nor courage lost, the while he faced
  Death and eternity!
The seething sea boiled o'er and o'er,
And hurled them on the flowery shore!

"O waken, waken, darling mine,
  Our pleasant home we 've found ;
Was never land like this divine,
  Nor such enchanting sound !
Was never shine of sun like this, —
Then ope thine eyes to sight of bliss !"

But, dead alike to joy or woe,
  She never moved again ;
Her face with smile was all aglow, —
  No look of fear or pain.
A hush fell down from sky on sea,
And dewy night wept mournfully.

Prostrate the knight sank by her side,
  Alone on stranger shore ;
Tears washed away his daring pride,
  Dissolved it evermore.
Before the image of her, dead,
His reckless heart was softenèd.

Then, as from out a dream he rose,
  And meekly bowed his head:
For now another home he knows,
  Where never sail has led;
And, kneeling on the lonely sod,
He turned his chastened soul to God!

High up the rocks he buried her,
  And reared a cross above;
Put off his cloak of silk and fur,
  And e'en the sword he loved:
He clothed himself in dress of skin,
And built a hut to live within.

And there, where madly beats the sea
  Against the rocky reef,
In solitude, all manfully
  He struggles with his grief;
There has since many a year agone
Found rest, a home, and his loved one.

When, bold, the sailor ventures nigh
  The lovely island shore,
He sees the cross there planted high,
  A warning evermore;
And oft the pious story 's told
Of him who placed it there of old.

WINTER SONG.

EICHENDORFF.

I DREAMT that I stood once again
  Before my father's door,
And gazed across the verdant vale
  Where oft I'd played before.
Soft kissed the perfumed wind my cheek,
  Fresh from the od'rous bowers;
And on my head and breast fell sweet
  A rain of fragrant flowers.

When I awoke, the moon's pale ray
  Faint shone above the wood,
A yellow light around me lay, —
  I knew not where I stood;

And as I sadly gazed around,
  It rained no blossoms there ;
Shroud-like the snow enwrapt the ground,
  And snow-white was my hair.

LONG AGO.

EICHENDORFF.

'TIS not the well-remembered tree,
  Beneath whose shade I used to stand,
And gaze as far as eye could see
  Across the fair and flowery land.

'T is not the ancient forest wide,
  That sang so sweetly in the wind,
Where oft I rode by her dear side,
    In trancèd revery of mind.

'T is not the sweet embowered dell,
  Where stately deer in safety stalked,
And where with her I loved so well
  At eve I often walked and talked.

Vale, wood, and tree unchanged remain,
  Earth wears the bloom it wore before :
Thou, older grown, art not the same,
  Thy blissful days of love are o'er !

COLUMBUS.

LOUISE BRACHMANN.

"WHAT is 't, Fernando? in thy frighted face
  Some dreadful tidings I can read!"
"Ah, noble master! seek God's saving grace;
  No more the crew my orders heed;
If soon th' expected land does not appear,
  They claim you for a sacrifice;
With furious oaths, all bounds o'erleaped, they swear
  That their most noble leader dies!"

And ere the knight the dreaded word had said,
  The crew, with terror mad, rushed in:
As when a storm, long threat'ning overhead,
  Bursts with a loud and horrid din,

So they, tumultuous, in the cabin crowd,
  Death in their looks, and wild despair:
"Traitor! where now are all thy hopes so proud?
  Or save us, or to die prepare!

"For food we 've often asked in vain; now blood,
  Your blood, we mean to have instead!"
Undaunted there the master calmly stood,
  Confronting them, and mildly said:
"Will blood appease ye, mine I gladly yield;
  But once more let me see the sun,
Through the dun mists of early morn revealed,
  Proclaim another day begun.

"If land greet not your longing eyes and mine,
  Then with me do whatso ye please!
But be of better cheer, to faith incline;
  Within his hand God holds the seas!"
Somewhat the master's words and looks serene
  Their rage allay, their fears beguile;

They move away with fierce and threat'ning mien,
And suffer him to live awhile.

"So be it then, if on to-morrow's morn
We do not sight the promised land;
Thy last look take upon the smiling dawn;
Then surely falls th' avenging hand!"
Thus, th' unfeeling, cruel compact made,
The heartless sailors turned aside.
The early beam of morn that gilds the wave
Their leader's fate will quick decide.

Blood-red the sun behind the sea sank down;
Night found Columbus sore oppressed;
The shudd'ring keel through boiling waves ploughed on,
And shook the foam from off its breast:
The sky with countless soft-eyed stars was bright,
But dark the master's aching soul,

Where no hope-star pierced through the dreary night,
  To guide him to the wished-for goal.

All night he watched with weary, anxious eye,
  An outlaw from the realms of sleep:
All night he saw the laggard hours go by,
  And heard the ocean's restless sweep.
"O speed thee westward, westward, trusty ship,
  As speeds the arrow from the bow!
My eager soul would time and distance skip,
  For westward must be land, I know!

"And Thou, O God! protect my suff'ring crew
  From all the dangers of the deep;
All the wild madness of their hearts subdue,
  And this good ship in safety keep!"
Thus as the night wore on, the master prayed:
  But hark! a hurried step is heard,—
Fernando, pale and sad, with look dismayed:
  Alas! he brings no cheering word.

"God help thee, master! night its round has
 run,
 Already breaks the dreadful dawn!"
"Be calm, my friend! who bids th' obedient sun
 Assist the feeble step of morn?
His will be done, though He should point my
 way
 Adown the darksome vale of death!"
"Farewell! farewell! O dreary, dreary day,
 That robs my noble lord of breath!"

And ere the knight the mournful word had said,
 The crew, with fury mad, rushed in:
As when a storm, long threat'ning overhead,
 Bursts with a loud and crashing din,
So they, tumultuous, in the cabin pour.
 "Yes, do with me whatso ye will;
But know, to westward lies the long-sought
 shore:
 May God preserve ye from all ill!"

Outleaped their gleaming swords, and a wild cry
  Upon the morning air rang out:
The master quietly prepared to die ;
  Resigned, he breathed a prayer devout.
No hallowed bond restrained th' impious band,
  They dragged him to the vessel's side ;
When from the mast-head came the cry of "Land!"
  And "Land!" a hundred mouths replied.

A faint, low line of purpling hue was seen ;
  Each moment more distinct it grew ;
And as the sun streamed out in golden sheen,
  Uprose the gleam of Hope anew :
While round the leader, pointing to the land,
  The land he said that they must find,
Was grouped, with claspèd hands, a tearful band,
  Awe-struck before his master mind!

DAWN.

MORIKE.

NO sleep has blessed my weary eyes,
Yet now I see the day-god rise,
  Darting his beams of light.

My anxious soul is tossed about,
Perplexed with many a fearful doubt ;
  Wan spectres haunt my sight.

    O soul, find peace !
From all thy night-long torture cease !
Rejoice ! I hear o'er vale and dell
The glad'ning notes of matin-bell !

HOPE.

GAUDY.

HOPE slumbers in the heart,
As in lily-cups the dew ;
Hope brightens, as the sun
Sparkles after storm anew ;
Hope blossoms, hardy flower,
In a heart cold as the grave ;
Hope smiles through all our tears,
As a gem beneath the wave.

And thus the human heart,
Often worsted and deceived,
To heaven turns afresh,
Where its woes may be relieved ;

As Arachne, never tired,
Spins her toilsome web again,
Though cruel hand of Fate
Make her task forever vain.

ON THE SILESIAN MOUNTAINS.

FREILIGRATH.

"HOW fragrant bloom the hedge-rows high,
And there's a daisy blossoming!
The ouzel and the bulfinch fly
Above their nests, and sweetly sing.
On silent feet the snow has fled,
Save where the mountains touch the sky;
In secret from the house I sped;
Here is the spot, now let me try: —
Rübezahl! *

* Rübezahl, or "Number Nip," is a mountain demon who, according to the legend, often gives help to the poor who call him. In the following poem, a boy, the son of a poor linen-weaver, thus invokes his aid.

"He did not hear! I'm not afraid,
He never did poor boy a wrong.
The piece of linen there I've laid,
I measured it; 't is very long:
I chose the finest I could find,
And father spins the best of all.
Ah, Rübezahl, be not unkind!
Once more the name I'll boldly call:—
Rübezahl!

"No answer yet! I sought the wood,
In hopes his succor to entreat!
My mother starves for want of food,
In all the house no bread to eat;
And father finds no one to buy
The cloth he spins the best of all.
What Rübezahl will do, I'll try;
Why comes he not? once more I'll call:—
Rübezahl!

"To many a poor one aid he lends:
Did not my granny tell me so?
He 's good to those who have no friends,
Who live in penury and woe.
That 's why I came to seek him here,
And brought the finest cloth we 've spun;
O he will buy, I need not fear, —
Come, Rübezahl! O please do come!
Rübezahl!

"If he should like the bundle there,
Perchance should say, 'Bring more, my lad!'
That would be nice, so nice; but where
Is more such linen to be had?
No matter, all is his at home,
If but his choice on this should fall;
Then all we 've pawned again we 'll own, —
O thought delicious! Rübezahl!
Rübezahl!

"Then home again I 'd wend my way;
'Gold, father, father!' I would call.
No more then would he curse, and say,
'I 'd better weave a shroud for all!'
And mother, she would smile again,
And never more for food we 'd pine;
And brothers, they would shout amain; —
O Rübezahl, once be benign!
Rübezahl!"

So called the simple-hearted child,
So stood, and called he, pale and faint:
In vain: within the Gnome-realm wild,
He only heard the ring-dove's plaint;
And while he watched, the day had flown,
In night's embrace the wood was clasped.
At last, in trembling undertone,
He sobbed, the while his tears fell fast, —
"Rübezahl!"

Night settled down so solemn, drear,
The lad, affrighted, screamed, "Hilloh!"
The bundle seized, and, pale with fear,
Went slowly back, heart-full of woe;
And by the wayside oft he laid
The bundle, to get breath again.
Erelong his shroud the father made,
From what was offered you in vain,
Rübezahl!

AUTUMN.

LENAU.

'TIS autumn, and the woods bewail
 The loss of all their leafy pride;
The joys of spring, the nightingale,
 I miss, as o'er the sea I glide.

The sky above is fair to view,
 But all its pleasant warmth is gone;
There 's no bloom on the waters blue,
 The blust'ring winds blow cold and long.

In sorrow flies my youth away,
 On spring's departing fragrant breath;
I shiver on this autumn day;
 My soul is sad, and dreams of death.

RETROSPECTION.

SCHWAB.

AT twenty, I lay dreaming,
In yonder forest there :
To-day I see it, seeming
As fresh and green and fair.
Its winds waft perfume hither,
Its brooks are brawling thither ;
Yes, 't will be young fore'er !

With man's step, firmer, bolder,
Once more I wander lone ;
In thought and purpose older,
In soul, too, older grown.
Ah, yes ! I must avow it,
With pain I must avow it,
On wings my youth has flown !

These sturdy oaks and beeches,
  With roots that intertwine,
Their arms stretched in far reaches,
  Like me, thought not of Time.
Like yonder cliffs, I ever
Thought Time must last forever,
  That it was wholly mine.

I am the same no longer,
  The woods the same remain ;
I am a restless wand'rer,
  'Gainst fate I strive in vain!
O, sadly blow the winds, alas!
Sadly through the gloom I pass :
  Would I were young again!

THE EMPEROR MAX AND ALBRECHT DURER.

FISCHER.

THE emperor Max, in silk and gold,
And velvet cloak (the story 's old),
And minister and council, go
To Albrecht Dürer's studio.
The artist by the hand he took,
And asked him with beseeching look,
If he would undertake to make
A picture for his emperor's sake.
The artist 'gan his paints to stir,
Which pleased all save the minister.

And 'fore the easel Dürer stood, —
No hand more skilful ever could

Make canvas more with beauty glow ;
For scarce a moment passed, and lo !
There pictured was sky, sea, and land;
Rare flowers fringed the ocean's strand ;
And clouds on clouds, in masses high,
Of sunset hues, hung in the sky ;
Rich plumaged birds swam i' the air.
Instinct with life, the picture there
Confessed a master's skill and care.

Loud was the emperor in his praise,
As down the brush the artist lays ;
Besought him Max : "O master mind,
Complete the work e'en now divine,
Until the ev'ning glow shall spread,
The landscape o'er, its hue of red."
"Fain thy behest I would obey,
So far as in my power lay,
But there is no one here to hold
The ladder, while I do as told."

"Hoho! if that be all you need,
There 's plenty here to help indeed.
How now, my lord, what troubles thee?
In no good humor seem'st to be?
Come, hold the ladder 'gainst the wall,
Thou art the strongest one of all."

When thus the emperor had said,
The frighted lord bowed low his head:
"In all thy court, no heart more true,
My liege and sov'reign, beats for you;
But O, I beg you will not ask
Me to perform this hateful task.
A nobleman cannot endure
To hold a ladder for this poor
And shabby churl, e'en though he be
An artist of celebrity."

Whereat the emperor, frowning, cried:
"Indeed! wherefore dost thus deride

Our aged friend, the artist, say?
Why dost thou treat him in this way?
Now listen: he is nobler than,
Far nobler than a nobleman.
No king or court creates his right,
But genius made it his birthright.
A grant of rank we can confer
On any boor, and dub him Sir;
But all the kings in Christendom
An artist cannot make, not one.
Of paint and canvas there 's great store,
Who bids it glow with beauty o'er?
Much brass and marble too have we,
Who breathes therein vitality?
What rank or title can compare
With godlike skill of Dürer there?

"Up, sir, the ladder hold, we say!
Now, noble master, paint away."

THE STARS OF THE NIGHT.

ARNDT.

THE sun had harnessed his coursers to ride
Round the world,
When the stars spake up: "We 'll go by thy side
Round the world."
But the sun roared forth: "Not one of ye go!
I 'll burn out your eyes with my fiery glow,
As I follow my course round the world!"

And the stars, abashed, sought the moon with sighs,
In the night;
And timidly said; "O Queen of the skies
In the night,
Let us go with thee, for thy gentle beam
Will never extinguish our golden gleam."
And she took them, companions of night!

O moon, and O stars! ye are welcome to me,
　　In the night!
What is hid in the heart, ye only may see
　　In the night!
Then kindle the lamps in yon azure dome,
While I wander on afar and alone, —
All alone with the beautiful night!

DEATH.

WACKERNAGEL.

BOY, pluck me flowers, cull me, oh,
The fairest that in gardens grow,
A wreath prepare.
Do we not deck the silent dead
With flowers fair?

I know once felt this breast of mine
The little joy that now is thine,
And all thy woe:
Once passion's stormy sea o'erflowed
This heart, I know.

O, 't was a subtle, magic tie,
That bound me down to life, and I
Am pris'ner yet:

The end is but deferred, — my heart
Release will get.

My spirit, where? — long since it fled;
And where my pride? — 't is withered, dead;
Worn out am I.
The last day dawns; why loiter here?
'T is time to die!

Yes, pluck me flowers, cull me, oh,
The fairest that in gardens grow;
A wreath prepare.
Do we not deck the silent dead
With flowers fair?

LOVE-SONG.

STERNAU.

I WANDER alone by the banks of the stream,
In the heart of the forest so deep;
"O tell me, fair stream, you can tell me I ween, —
Why must I sorrow and weep?"
The wavelets are murmuring softly and low,
As they flow on their way to the sea;
Forever are murmuring softly and low,
But have never an answer for me!

The wind blows its breath on the early-born flow'rs,
And strews them along my sad way:
"O tell me, ye blossoms, fair emblems of lovers,
Why should I sorrow this day?"
The birds half unclosing their roseate eyes,
Which are wet with sad tears I can see,

Gaze lovingly at me while bursting with sighs,
  But have never an answer for me!

"O bird of the woodland, so tenderly chanting
  A happy love-lay to thy mate,
Cease thy sweet music, and tell me lamenting,
  Why should I weep at my fate?"
He stops and he listens, flies nearer to listen,
  No more may he sing in his glee,
But is mournfully silent,—ah, touchingly silent,
  And has never an answer for me!

As I wander alone in the midnight afar,
  In the silence of midnight so deep:
"I beseech thee, O tell me, thou silvery star,
  Why do I sorrow and weep?"
But the star, it is voiceless, and pale in the sky;
  I hear but the moan of the sea.
Stream, flower, and bird, and yon planet on high,—
  They have never an answer for me!

THE TWIN SONG.

REINECK.

A BIRD sits where the roses blow,
In the silver, summer night;
A maid sits in the grass below,
In the silver, summer night.
If the maid sing, the bird must hear;
If the bird sing, the maid gives ear;
And afar may be heard,
Now maid, now bird,
As the echoes in vale and grove are stirred.

What sang the bird to the zephyr air,
Of the silver, summer night?
What sang the maid to the moon so fair,
Of the silver, summer night?

O, the bird sang of the spring-tide bright;
O, the maid sang of young love's delight;
　　How the echoes prolong
　　Their lovely song,
Ne'er can I forget through all my life long!

THE YOUTH BY THE BROOK.

SCHILLER.

WHERE the waters welled, a stripling
  Sat, and pulled a wreath apart;
And he watched the torn leaves swiftly
  Down the dancing ripples dart:
"Thus my wingèd days speed onward,
  Like the wavelets, fleetly by;
Thus my youthful moments wither,
  Like the flowerets, quickly die!

"Ask me not wherefore I sorrow
  In the bloom-time of my years;
There is hope and joyance ever,
  When the budding spring appears:
But these many thousand voices
  Nature utters, born again

In the deeps of my lone bosom,
  Waken only woe and pain.

" Ne'er may these joys make me joyous,
  Though spring all its wealth display,
One there is, but one, I long for,
  Near she is, yet far away.
Ardently my arms outstretching,
  Would I clasp the fleeting form;
Vainly, for I cannot reach it,
  E'er my heart is lone and lorn!

" O descend, thou fairest, dearest!
  Leave thy proud height, and come down!
Flowerets, first born of the spring-time,
  Shall be woven for thy crown!
List to Philomel's sweet singing,
  List the waters' rippling flow;
E'en the lowliest hut 's a dwelling
  Eden-like, where love does glow!"

THE KING OF THULÉ.

GOETHE.

TO Thulé's faithful monarch brave,
(None more than he could dare,)
His dying queen a goblet gave,
All golden, rich, and rare.

Naught valued he above the cup;
From it alone drank he:
Whene'er at feast he took it up,
His eyes filled tearfully.

And when death unrelenting came
To call the monarch home,
He gave away his crown, his name,
But kept the cup alone.

And seated in th' ancestral hall,
  In his castle by the sea,
He called around his nobles all, —
  A lordly company.

Then rose the aged monarch up:
  "Farewell to earth, to grief!"
He drank, — then tossed the cherished cup
  Into the wave beneath.

He watched it fill, and sink from sight
  Deep in the swelling sea;
Then closed his eyes in death's long night:
  Ne'ermore a drop drank he!

NIGHT SONG.

MEISZNER.

THOU raging stream, thou gloomy vale,
Ye wake again
In my sore breast the olden wail,
The olden pain.

As here the stream, in thunder-tone,
Roars down the rocks,
Bursts through the heart the fearful moan
Of passion's shocks.

As here, 'mid bleak and barren mounts,
A vulture moans,
Through all the heart's deserted founts,
The old grief groans.

O, bear the fate that falls to thee!
    Imagine not
Another joyous spring to see;
    Not such thy lot!

Hug not the vain idea, that soon
    Thine eyes may see
Thy fatherland, whence cruel doom
    Has exiled thee.

Nor stoop again thy cross to kiss,
    Now borne so long;
Bid grief cease, and thine only bliss
    End thy last song.

O raging stream! O gloomy vale!
    Ye wake again
In my sore breast the old, old wail,
    The old, old pain!

THE HAPPY DEATH.

STÖBER.

ON the banks of sunny Rhine,
A fisher's hut you see:
"Come, O darling maiden mine,
Maiden mine,
Come forth, come forth to me!"

"I will gladly come to thee,
Will meet thee at the gate.
Storm can never frighten me,
Frighten me,
If I may share thy fate."

"O let nothing frighten thee!
Be life one happy dream:

Wilt thou only trust to me,
Trust to me,
My boat waits in the stream."

Now into the boat they leap,
It flies before the blast:
'Mid the roar of thunders deep,
Thunders deep,
They clasp each other fast.

Lo! there came a lightning-stroke,
It struck, alas! the pair;
Farewell, — the lovers awoke,
They awoke,
In realms of Heaven fair!

On drave the quivering bark,
Adown the foaming tide;
With the lovers cold and stark,
Cold and stark,
Far out to ocean wide.

Now the storm has passed away,
Gone all the clouds so dark :
Where the waves swell, dashing spray,
Dashing spray,
Dances the coffin-bark.

THE VIOLET.

GOETHE.

A VIOLET in the woodland grew,
A modest flower, observed by few,
    A fragrant violet;
When came a fair young shepherd-maid,
With tripping step, in smiles arrayed,
    Adown, adown,
  The path adown, and sang.

"Alas!" the lovely flower began,
"Were I the fairest known to man,
    And not a violet;
Then might I please yon maiden's eye,
And pressed upon her bosom lie!
    That I, that I,
  The rose awhile might be!"

Alas! alas! the maiden trod
Unconscious o'er the flowery sod,
And crushed the violet!
It perished in a fragrant sigh:
"If die I must, through thee I die!
Through thee, through thee,
At thy belovèd feet!"

THE FLOWER.

FERRAND.

MY heart is a flower,
It blooms not to the sight ;
And when the storms of winter come,
It dreams of spring-tide bright.

My heart is a flower,
Exhaling fragrant breath ;
And if no passion bid it wake,
It sleeps, as though in death.

My heart is a flower ;
And when love makes it break,
Then only will it burst in bloom, —
In sunlight will awake !

THE SEXTON'S SONG.

HOELTY.

DIG, dig, O Spade!
Whate'er these sturdy hands have made,
  Good Spade, they owe to thee!
For rich and poor alike must come;
Sooner or later, every one
  Is brought at last to me!

  Whilom so proud,
Yon skull to fawning, flatt'ring crowd
  Scarce deigned a passing thank.
These bones that lie all scattered here
Belonged to one men held in fear,
  So great his power and rank.

Yon golden hair
Decked once the head of maid as fair
As ever angels are ;
And oft the lover's boastful tongue
Told of her loveliness among
Her rivals near and far.

Dig, dig, my Spade !
Whate'er these sturdy hands have made,
Good Spade, they owe to thee !
For rich and poor alike must come ;
Sooner or later, every one
Is brought at last to me !

THE TOILETTE OF CONSTANCE.

CASIMIR DE LA VIGNE.

"HASTE, Anna, haste! the glass!
O haste! the hour will pass!
To-night, you know, I mean to dance
At the Ambassador's of France.

"Ah, see those bows! how faded there!
Bright yesterday! Time robs us all!
Look! from the net that binds my hair,
Graceful the golden acorns fall.

"And on my brow this jewel bright; —
Don't hurt me so! You are so dull!
Not there; yes, here; ah, that is right! —
My dear, am I not beautiful?

"He whom I vainly would forget
(Anna, my dress) I hope to see.

No, I 'll not wear that amulet,
'T was blest by holy priest for me.
Ah me! if he should press my hand, —
The very thought takes breath away!
When in confessional I stand,
How dare I all that happened say?"

Before the grate she stopped to gaze, —
O God! a spark flew on her dress:
"Fire! help!" she ran; the fatal blaze,
Too swift, enwraps her loveliness;
It clasps, and with voluptuous breath
Glows o'er and round her, pitiless.
Woe 's me! so fair, and such a death,
In such a dream of happiness!

Farewell pleasure, love, and ball!
They only said, "Ah, poor Constance!"
Till dawn, dance-music filled the hall,
At the Ambassador's of France.

VERSES.

RETROSPECTION.

AR away I hear
The murmur of the summer sea
Upon the summer sands.
Wave after wave breaks gently on the shore,
And dies away to softly sigh once more.

Ships upon the sea
Are ladened not with richer freight
Than these waves bring to me.
The ceaseless music of their plaintive roll
In soft enchantment holds my dreaming soul.

From some Æolian harp,
Wooed softly by the zephyr air,
Float breaths of boyhood's song.

The well-remembered strains fall on my ears,
And flood my pensive soul with passionate tears.

Some memory of yore
With ev'ry wave-sigh comes to me, —
Some face I knew before;
And long-lost thoughts crowd in upon my brain,
That tell me of my vanished youth again.

O days of youth misspent!
That ye should ever come and go
Like wavelets of the sea!
Ye creep apace along the sands of Time,
And leave our passive lives without a sign!

The glory of the year
Is seen in orchard and in field,
At autumn, brown and sere;
But o'er manhood's prime, that dark and dreary sea,
A waste of waves is washing ceaselessly!

ANGLING SONGS.

I.

WHEN murm'ring wakes the summer wind
To ope the pearly gates of dawn,
With tranquil mind,
Let me prepare
To angle where
Yon river rolls its tide along,
O'er rocks and silver sands in gentle song.

Ye slumb'ring flowers, haste to drip
Your fragrant stores of honeyed dew,
The bee may sip:
Ye fields of corn,
To greet the morn

Your slender, em'rald arms unfold,
And joyous bow your tasselled plumes of gold!

And ye, sweet choristers of air,
Begin the anthem to the day
That dawns so fair ;
By dancing rills
'Mid whispering hills,
Chant the glad chorus of the hour,
From leafy covert and from scented bower.

Mine eye feasts on this Eden scene,
Mine ear to soft enchantment yields ;
The while I dream,
And silent try,
With painted fly,
The timid trout to deftly snare,
Or lure the greedy pike from out his lair.

O ye, who toil in busy towns,
And wear out life in anxious strife,

List to the sounds
That bid ye here
Where God is near;
And nature sings with siren voice,
"Come, walk with me, and evermore rejoice!"

II.

O MORNING fair!
Like rain of diamonds on the dewy lawn
Thy soft beams fall;
And everywhere
I hear the call
Of myriad voices from their leafy lair,
To wake and bid a welcome to the dawn.

The bee, on fleet,
Industrious wing, now takes his flight away;
Intent to sip,

From chalice, meet
For elfin lip,
The overflowing store of honey sweet ;
Pure incense offered to the opening day.

As one a-dream
The restless river frets within its bed,
While arrow-like,
Across the stream,
The darting flight
Of swallow lightly skims the rippled gleam,
And song of lark is fainting overhead.

The sweet south-wind,
All fragrant from the dew-bedripping flowers,
Comes with quick feet
And loving mind,
The stream to greet.
The wave 's expectant, coy, but not unkind ;
And there, in dalliance soft, they pass the hours.

Good fortune mine,
That thus propitious grants so fair a day!
With joy I see
The signs benign,
And eagerly,
Once more equipped with trusty rod and line,
To yonder rock and river wend my way.

SONNETS.

I.

WHERE fair Meaumee flows its banks atween,
Kissing the moss-grown roots that fringe its edge,
Or where, with quickened pace, the ripples gleam,
As down the rocks they leap from ledge to ledge,
How oft the sunny summer days I 've spent,
Free as the unimprisoned wind that blew,
With line to snare the finny tribe intent,
As happy as the bird that by me flew!
And with me one, an old and cherished friend,
Not less a lover of the gentle art,
In whom most happily I found to blend
The noblest attributes of head and heart.
Long may we thus our happy sport pursue,
And time waste all, but this joy e'er renew!

II.

A curious web of tangled lines it shows,
This twisted thorn, with half its roots revealed,
Behind whose slanting trunk I stand concealed,
And angle in the stream that 'neath me flows.
For here, in schools, the keen-eyed bass await,
In steady balance poised upon the tide,
The quiet dropping of the tempting bait,
With deadly skill prepared for deadlier fate ;
Scarce seems the limpid stream to flow at all,
The only sound the wood-dove's plaintive call ;
Around me, everywhere, a sea of corn,
Each emerald blade bedewed with tears of morn :—
A spring ! a splash ! and, flouncing on the sward,
The patient angler claims his great reward !

THE ANGLERS.

FED from its springs, the rains have overflowed,
What time the creek expansive rolls along,
Now in a broad, unbroken, watery sweep,
Then, rushing through a channel, narrow, deep,
Impatient of its too-confinèd banks, —
I reel my stoutest line, in hopes to take
The noblest fish, now tempted to forsake
His hiding-place beneath the sunken roots,
In greedy range abroad his prey to seek.
The turbid waters now no image show,
To fright the finny tribe that dwells below;
So needs the angler no projecting trunk
Of overhanging tree his form to hide,
But boldly walk the wave-washed shore he may,
Intent alone to watch the sudden spring,

That almost jerks his straining line away ;
Nor seen, nor seeing, but with pole in hand,
He feels the fish, who sometimes toys awhile,
And sometimes, with a cunning unsurpassed,
The bait secures, but 'scapes the fatal guile ;
Yet often skill and patience win the day,
And numerous prizes well the toil repay.

When, blazing in the cloudless vault above,
The sun one half his daily course has run,
And Ploughman, passing on his way to dine,
Stops to ask what luck attends my line:
" The big fish ought to bite to-day," he says,
" No use to try them when the creek is clear."
Then seek I out some sheltered, grassy nook,
And, tired, put away awhile my hook ;
First count the well-earned trophies of the morn,
Admiring, as I range them on the lawn ;
Then spread the frugal meal I 've brought, and bid
My friend, still loitering by the stream, to come.

With what good appetite we linger here,
And what digestion waits upon us near,
Ask him who loves to wander by the stream,
And all its various, devious windings trace;
Who knows the haunts and habits of the tribe
That gleaming 'neath the waters sportive glide;
'Fore whom the book of Nature open lies,
His heart expanding, while it glads his eyes:
Go ask the patient angler, and decline
To deem him idle, while he wanders on.
God's utterance is in the whisp'ring woods,
And may be heard aright by one whose moods,
Attuned to heavenly harmonies like these,
Are in divine accord with all he sees.

Stretched on the velvet sward, at ease, we pass,
My friend and I, a pleasant hour in talk.
Our theme is angling; and in turn 't is told
When and where was caught the largest bass;
Or else, in argumentative debate,

We lose ourselves in labyrinth of speech,
As wise at last as when we first began,
For never to conclusion can we reach ;
Or while the chirping birds and squirrels clean
The remnants of our sylvan feast away,
With joyous song we pull the feathered oar ;
Or, musing, let the boat drift down the stream.
This little song, writ by the kind old man,
Now dead, who taught us first how best to fling
The fly where timid trouts to rise began,
Is one I always ask my friend to sing.

I.

O wind of the summer morn !
Waken the wave asleep,
The dreamy wave asleep ;
While down th' accustomed path I go,
To the willow that overhangs the flow
Of waters dark and lorn.

II.

O clouds of the azure sky!
Arise to greet the morn,
The dewy, fragrant morn.
In glad procession meet the day,
Now breaking there in bright array,
With hues of matchless dye.

III.

O lark of the tuneful throat!
Wend heavenward thy flight,
Thy spiral, vocal flight.
Aneath this graceful willow-tree
I 'll cast my line, and patiently
Attend my dancing float.

IV.

O lamp of the summer night!
Low in the western sky,
The golden evening sky:
Guide my faltering footsteps home,
While mem'ry treasures for its own
A day of calm delight.

And so we while the idle hour away.
For, till the sun begins, with tempered heat,
Adown the western wall of heaven to creep,
'T is vain to tempt the sluggish finny race,
Refusing now to leave their hiding-place.
Not e'en the choicest bait that you may throw
Can make them quit the quiet depths below;
For there, full-fed, perchance asleep, they lie
Secure, and all the angler's arts defy.

But when, with loitering step, the sunlight leaves
The lawn, o'er which the lengthening shadows creep,
Then have we mind no more to talk or row,
But, armed again with rod and slender line,
Our meditative art once more we ply,
Where foaming down the rocks the waters leap,
Or where between the trees they calmly flow.
One spot there is, midway adown the stream,
A quiet pool, o'er whose dark water hangs

A canopy of pliant beechen boughs :
Some point erect towards the sky above,
Some, pendent, sweep the liquid floor below ;
Around the curvèd banks thick grasses grow,
O 'er all an emerald net the ivy throws.
Here, in the quiet of the vernal eve,
Completely hidden from the outward world,
(Such is the silence of the time and place,)
I watch my float, and linger, loath to leave
The foolish fancies that my brain doth weave.

The too fleet-footed day has fled, — and Night,
The weird witch, Night, spreads with her stealthy
hand
O'er all a black veil gemmed with twinkling stars;
Dark falls the deepening shadow on the land,
And slowly fades the landscape from my sight ;
The wind its listless arms has dropped, — a hush
Of perfect quiet all enfolds, — nor sound,
Except the murmuring of the stream, is heard,

Or cry of owl, night's melancholy bird.
We slowly wend our way, well laden, home.
No moon we need to guide our tardy step
Along the river's bank, and through the wood.
The beaten path our feet have learned to know,
So often have we trod it to and fro.

The day is ended, and my song is done.
Let others choose the pleasures they like best;
Be mine the angler's joys,—his peace of mind,
His converse with the woods and purling streams,—
And mine the happy fancies of his dreams.

THE ANGLER'S SONG.

ONCE more I tread thy pebbly shore,
Fair brook!
And view the scenes I saw lang syne,
Accoutred, as so oft before,
With tapering rod and silken line
And barbèd hook.

The mill dilapidated stands;
And see
Its moss-grown wheel, forever still,
All choked with weed and drifting sands,
O'er which the water's dancing rill
Made melody.

There, where the overhanging tree
Bends low,
The naiad of the brook to woo,
Patient, — from care and trouble free, —
How oft the fatal snare I threw,
Long days ago!

Again I angle in the pool,
Or troll
The ripples' murm'ring, eddying flow;
The while the sweet south-wind doth cool
The sultry heat of noontide's glow,
As on I stroll.

What though successless, still I fish
And wait;
And still the winding brooklet trace.
No happier pastime might I wish,
Than thus to tempt the finny race,
And meditate!

THE ANGLER'S WALK.

ATHROUGH the dim cathedral wood,
Adown its leafy aisles,
Ere breaks the sunlight through the roof in smiles,
I walk in musing mood.

A silence deep enwraps me round,
My step is scarcely heard ;
When lo ! I hear the notes of morning bird
Pour forth harmonious sound.

And while the music stirs the air
I see the morn arise ;
On either side the solemn forest lies
In vernal beauty there.

I watch the squirrel gambol free,
The morning glories ope,
And, curious, pause in almost earnest hope
To hear what says the tree.

And yonder, where the woodland ends,
Athrough the leaves I see
The quiet river, as around the lea
In silver line it bends.

With quickened step I seek its edge,
And find the well-known spot
Where crocus, and the meek forget-me-not,
Half hid, bloom in the sedge.

For there alone I've angled long,
With varied fortune oft,
Where rippling waves and winds that whispered soft
Sang their melodious song.

Whene'er the trees renew their green,
And river melts its chain,
Ere dawn of day I pass the wood a-dream,
And angle there again.

CANZONÉTTA.

BY day I think of thee,
At night I dream of thee ;
And all the wingèd hours,
Bring memories of thee, —
Sweet memories to me.

The language of thine eyes,
The music of thy words,
That fell upon my soul
Like songs of summer birds.

The sunlight of thy face,
Thy happy, radiant face,
Looks so fraught with meaning,
Acts so rich in grace ;
These indeed are treasures,

Pearls of cherished thought;
O intoxicating thought!
Dear indeed the pleasures
Thy memory has brought!

Cambridge: Printed by Welch, Bigelow, and Company.

www.ingramcontent.com/pod-product-compliance
Lightning Source LLC
LaVergne TN
LVHW021407110826
845150LV00007B/1816

9781425512804